Galina, All About Love

Youssef Khalim

Copyright © 2013 Youssef Khalim

All rights reserved.

ISBN: **978- 0-9787798-9-4**
ISBN-13: 978-0978779894

DEDICATION

To: Lori (The real or ideal soul mate: inspiration)

            Tonya Tracy Khalim and

            Runako Soyini Khalim, (my most beloved daughters)

            Mother and Grandmother and Great-grandmother, (my most beloved maternal biological ancestors, and spiritual antecedents)

            M. A. Garvey (one of my 7 M's: my role models)

            Youssef Khalim II; III (my most beloved sons)

            Father and Grandfather and Great-grandfather, (my most beloved paternal biological ancestors, and spiritual antecedents)

To: The Forerunners and Reincarnation sources (beloved biological ancestors and spiritual antecedents), and

            The Almighty (our Spiritual Father), from whence we come.

CONTENTS

	Acknowledgments	i
1	Introduction	1
2	You Gave Me Your Body	Pg 2
3	I Love To Take a Stroll With You	Pg 3
4	I Thought About You All Day Long	Pg 4
5	You Are the Perfect Woman	Pg 5
6	You Put A Smile On My Face!	Pg 6
7	You Are My Fantasy!	Pg 7
8	You & Me	Pg 9
9	You Are the Most Beautiful	Pg 10
10	How We Know That God Exists	Pg 11
11	You Take My Breath Away!	Pg 12
12	You Are Divine	Pg 13
13	Want To Play?	Pg 14
14	I've Never Wanted Someone	Pg 15
15	You Know How To Make Me Happy	Pg 16
16	Sexy To The Core	Pg 17
17	Autumn Is So Much Fun With You	Pg 18
18	You Are Very, Very Special	Pg 19
19	Princess Galina, Among the Silver Birch	Pg 20
20	Yoga	Pg 22

21	We Are Possessed	Pg 24
22	You Are a Master in the Art Of Love	Pg 25
23	Somewhere In Heaven?	Pg 26
24	In Case You Ever About It	Pg 27
25	I Love You More	Pg 28
26	All About Love	Pg 29
27	You Are The Most	Pg 31
28	About The Author, And Other Books	Pg 32

ACKNOWLEDGMENTS

To: The Forerunners and Reincarnation sources (beloved biological ancestors and spiritual antecedents), and

The Almighty (our Spiritual Father), from whence we come.

1 INTRODUCTION

I was born December 25, 1979, in a small village, near Minsk, Belarus. I have been told that I am logical, rational, and intelligent. However, my friends say it is great fun to be around me because I sometimes joke around, and have a good sense of humor.

I became interested in modeling in Belarus, and I intend to pursue it as a major goal. I am 5'6" tall, and I weigh 110 pounds. I have green eyes. Currently, I work in an office in Minsk. My dream, later, is to marry and have children.

Galina,
August 21, 2004

Galina, All About Love is the third in a series of eight books by Youssef Khalim, begun in 2002. Four were inspired by ladies encountered over- seas. Galina is one of the four overseas encounters.

I met Galina in the summer of 2004, over the Internet. I saw her photo on New-Dating.Com, and e-mailed her. Later, I was struck by her extraordinary beauty and lovely personality. I wrote down my feelings, thoughts, and moods as fast as I could. In essence, Galina is the motivation and inspiration for this book. Sometimes it seemed that the book was writing itself, and I was only a channel, trying to keep up.

First, came *You Gave Me Your Body*. Then, the other selections followed rapidly, and the book was complete in 18 days, working part time.

Galina has the most gorgeous, sexy body, and attractive and charismatic personality, and I have attempted to capture and reflect her awesome presence and personality in *Galina, All About Love*.

And now I present to you the exciting, electric, and exotic *Galina*.

Youssef Khalim,
8/21/04

2 YOU GAVE ME YOUR BODY

You Gave Me Your Body

And,

You gave us the world!

3 I LOVE TO TAKE A STROLL WITH YOU

Walk hand-in-hand,
And feel my arm around your waist,

Sit snugly by you in the grass,
And listen to your lovely voice,
And hear about your plans and goals,

Watch you deftly wield your sword, a blade of grass,
Run after you, and catch you,
And feel you wriggle, in my arms,
To get free,
Kiss your mouth, (a taste of heaven),
Hold you in my arms, and say, "I love you."

Watch you,
Lovely, in the swing,
Before we walk away together,
So we can be alone.

But first, I want to
Take a stroll with you.

4 I THOUGHT ABOUT YOU ALL DAY LONG

Your scented hair, disarming smile,
The way you laugh,
The way you gesture with your hands,
The way your hips move when you walk,
The way you snuggle up to me,
The way it feels to touch your skin,

How wonderful it is to soak myself in you,
I love you.

Fulfill your every wish and fantasy,
Love every inch of you,

And join our bodies
And our minds into one soul,

And turn all life to love,
All day long.

5 YOU ARE THE PERFECT WOMAN

Not only are you

The

Perfect Woman,

But you are the

Perfect Woman,

For me.

6 YOU PUT A SMILE ON MY FACE

Pep in my step
Kick in my knee,

You energize me,
Motivate me,
Focus me.

You give momentum,
Creativity,
Imagination;
Verve, vigor, vitality.
You give a different reality.

I love just thinking about you,

And loving you
Is like a dream come true.

You put a smile on my face, and pep in my step

For days.

7 YOU ARE MY FANTASY

My drug,
Intoxicant,
Stimulant,
Upper,
Oxygen,

My fix,
My pill,
Heaven's gift,
My joyful morning kiss,
My mystery lady, woman,
Human-growth Hormone,

You amaze and inspire me,
(And when I think of you, I *grow*)

You are my sweet, sweet drug of choice,
My dear;

My friend and lover,
Forever.

You are the one I love, adore.
More, and more, and more.

My daydream,
Nighttime fantasy!

Fantastic, fun,
You're hot!

You send me on a trip
Around the universe-
And back to you.

You are my angel, vamp, and diva,

Excitement! WOW!

In short, you are my lovely fantasy,
And
My dream
Come true.

8 YOU & ME

Your presence
& your spirit
Dip so gently
Into me:

Caress my body, mind, & soul;

Mingle with you,
Elevate me,

Arouse my better,
Inner,
POWERFUL

You,
& Me.

9 YOU ARE THE MOST BEAUTIFUL

Your attitude is
Correct:

You are *the*
Most
Beautiful
Woman

In the whole wide world.

10 HOW WE KNOW THAT GOD EXISTS

Life is everywhere,
And life exists in many forms,
Life is love,
So, love is everywhere,
And life is logical, rational, intelligent.
Love is always seeking a chance to manifest,
And, it is everywhere.

In higher levels of evolution,
Love is often felt as bliss, ecstasy, and joy.
At lower levels, it is the will to live.

"God" is love (and life),
So, God is everywhere,
(Throughout the universe, and is the "highest" level of being, or evolution).
You exist,
You are divine,
And loving, lovable,
And manifesting love.
(Because, life is love).
We met across a network made by rational minds,
For, by, and of love, because it was manifest destiny.
(A US thing).
So, love is the seeking, controlling factor here,
Destined to seek and give, share and care, boundless bliss, ecstasy, and joy.

It's clear, I love you,
With the greatest love that can exist.

We know for certain, love exists,
Love *is* God,
And therefore God exists.

11 YOU TAKE MY BREATH AWAY

When I look into your eyes,
And see the halo 'round your head,
And taste your mouth, and sample heaven,
And touch your skin, caressing celestial softness,
And see you walk, and watch the magic of the universe,

And hold you, love you, *totally*, completely,

And listen to your lovely voice,

And take you,
Just as nature takes its course,
On mountain peaks,
And grassy plains and valleys,
Flooding lakes and streams;
Bringing life, & love,

I take you.

And stars twinkle endlessly,
And take my breath away!

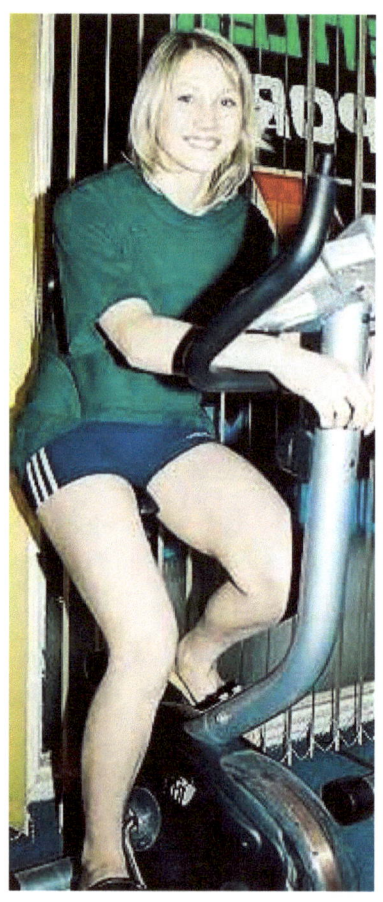

12 YOU ARE DIVINE

You are divinely beautiful,

Stunningly beautiful,

Drop-dead GORGEOUS!

Exotic, SEXY,

Incomparable,

Celestial,

Lovely,

Majestic,

Royal, noble,

Heavenly,

Warm and sweet:

Divine.

13 WANT TO PLAY?

I know you've had a long, hard day,
I wonder… if you'll rest, and want to play.

Said you were tired, and hungry,
Let me see…

Relax, and rest my love,
'Cause we're eating out tonight.

Let's start out with a sparkling wine,

Then salad, and your favorite dish,
And anything at all your lovely heart may wish,

After your meal, and music, I see you're moving to the beat.
Energized,
You excite, and mesmerize me.

Galina, you look so good tonight!

I'm happy to have you as my own,
And now, it's time for us to get back home.

I thank my lucky stars for you,
And *all* I ever want to do,
Is love you.

Now, back home, I run your bath,
Make mine for last,
Am waiting for your cue.

And all this time,
I wondering if you're rested,
And hoping you want to play.

14 MORE THAN ANYONE HAS LOVED BEFORE

What I really find strange is that I've never loved
Anyone more than I love you.

I've never wanted someone, more than I want you.

I never wanted to do, what I want with you.

I never wanted to fly, never wanted to soar,
I never wanted to dance, never wanted to roar.

I never wanted to kiss, never wanted to love,
And stay up all night long, and greet the Morning Dove.

I have never had so much pleasure,
Like you give beyond measure.

I want you, here, in my life,
Because *once* with you, is like *living twice*.

And I love you more,
Than anyone has ever loved before.

15 YOU KNOW HOW TO MAKE ME HAPPY

You know how to make me happy,
Melt my heart, and touch my soul.

You know how to energize me, motivate me,
Make me whole.

You know just how to love me,
Touch my mind, and make me smile.

As long as time continues,
I'll keep you by my side.

I love you when I think of you,
I love to hear your voice,

Out of this universe of ours,
You are my love of choice.

I love to hold you, touch, and take you,
Make you happy too.

I love you so much, Sweetheart,
'Cause you know just what to do.

You are my rainbow in the sky,
And this great love will never die.

You make me happy,
Touch my soul,

With you beside me, Baby,
At long last, I am whole.

16 SEXY TO THE CORE

I love how you are:

Shy, & coy, & modest,
Bold, brave, & fearless,
Open,
Adventurous,
Curious,
Intelligent,
Careful, cautious,
Frugal, & hard working,
Athletic,
Healthy,
EXOTIC,
Independent,
Playful,
Funny,
Fun,
Loving, lovable,
Beautiful, & lovely,
Exciting,
GORGEOUS,

&
SEXY to the core.

17 AUTUMN IS SO MUCH FUN WITH YOU

Your warmth replaces autumn's chill,
Your dress snugly hugs your curvy hips,
Your sweater glorifies your chest,

Your eyes are beautiful
Just like stunning autumn leaves,
You are reflected in the mirror of the lake.

I love autumn,
Because it's awesome!
Majestic!
Beautiful!
And fun!

Just like you.
And autumn is so much fun
This year,

With you here!

18 YOU ARE VERY, VERY SPECIAL

You are very special,
Very unique,
Very lovely,
Sweet, Warm, & Sexy.
You are very wonderful,
Very smart,
Delightfully engaging,
& lovable.
You are very, very special,
You are my very special treasure,
& I treasure you,
& cherish you,
With a very special
Love.

19 PRINCESS GALINA, AMONG THE SILVER BIRCH

I've been searching for you, all my life,
Was Cleopatra just another lover, or a future wife?

I searched the whole wide world for you,
And now, I found you, Golden Girl,

In the early evening, in the park
I found you, among the Silver Birch,

Perching on the verge of fame,
Your name in waiting,
The Universe prepared to sing your praises,
Celebrate you, crown you: Golden Galina, of Belarus,
The reigning Princess, over us.

Your name in waiting,
The Universe prepared to sing your praises,
Bestow on you grand accolades, and roses,
And love you madly, like I do.

Hold your warm hands, in the park,
Kiss you lightly, after dark.
And taste you sweetly, beneath the Silver Birch.

I'll take you, beneath the Silver Birch,
And love you, like God loves His church.

My Princess, and my greatest find,
And time will tell if you are mine,

And see if you are friend and lover,
Coming fully into my life.

Was Cleopatra just another lover, or a future wife?

Princess Galina, Among The Silver Birch

20 YOGA

I love practicing yoga
With you:

The headstands, leg-lifts,
All the various positions,

The seeking, universal love,
Unity of minds, bodies, souls.

And isn't Tantra totally cool?

You help me with my physical,
Spiritual, and soul development,
Sweetheart.

I love practicing yoga
With you:

And love you fully forever, even more than
The love we had at practice.

21 WE ARE POSSESSED

In loving you,
We take possession

Of each other's bodies, minds, spirits, and souls.

After loving you,
We are possessed-

Of each other.

22 YOU ARE A MASTER IN THE ART OF LOVE

When I come to see you,

You are always
Beautiful,
Lovely,

Charming,
Smiling,
Considerate,
Kind,
Intelligent, thoughtful,
Sweet,
Sexy,
Generous,
Funny,
Engaging, and
Supportive.

I marvel at your mastery.

And, my love for you just

Grows

By
Leaps and bounds,

Because,
You are the master
In the art of love.

23 SOMEWHERE IN HEAVEN?

To hold, and kiss the girl
You love,
Puts the man and woman
In heaven.

So, when I love you,
Must put us
Somewhere,
Elsewhere,
Wherever,
Where only *we* can go.

24 IN CASE YOU WONDER ABOUT IT:

You are the only woman for me.
And I love you,
Want you,
Need you,

And only you,
In my life
Forever.

25 I LOVE YOU MORE

I Love you

More

Than Mortals

Are allowed

To love.

26 ALL ABOUT LOVE

Come, my sweetheart.
Let us learn all about love:

Let us teach each other,
Learn from each other,
Share and care, with patience and acceptance;

Take long walks in-the-park;
Give a smile, and go a million miles to serve;

Take any measure to give you pleasure, joy, and bliss;

Kiss you softly,
Say, "I love you," ten million times;

Bring you heaven-scented tulips on just an ordinary day;

Give you Tantra, sing your mantra;
Love you every hour of every single day;

Pray for you, and serenade you.
Enjoy a joke, poke fun at irony;
Need you;

Share your hopes and your dreams,
Lift your burdens,
Make you beam;
Rock your world with passion,
Bring back the fashion
Of love;

Make children sure to please Creation,
Enjoy the best of all sensations;

Take on the devil, fight evil together;
Stand for truth, justice, Human Rights;

Protect our family and our home,
Know the difference between right from wrong,

Sing songs, and read together;
Ride our bikes along the winding trail of life;
Travel widely,
And

Take FULL responsibility for ALL the earth
And ALL mankind,

And prove to God that on this earth,
Some of us still know
All about love.

27 YOU ARE THE MOST

You are the most

Exciting

July 4th
Event

I ever

Had.

28 ABOUT THE AUTHOR, AND OTHER BOOKS

Youssef Khalim obtained Unity in yoga on about 7/20/80. He says, "We will recombine into one faith, Judaism, Christianity, and Islam." He has been able to "see" and experience some amazing information about USA presidents Jefferson, Lincoln, and Obama; and also Prophets Moses, Muhammad, and Solomon - in visions, lucid dreams, and in meditation. Khalim makes reincarnation (resurrection) central again in our western religions. He resides in the Chicagoland area. And he is the father of Tonya, Runako, and Noah. See his books on the following websites: http://amazon.com, http://lulu.com, and http://sunracommunications.com

OTHER BOOKS

Youssef Khalim's books include *People Of The Future/Day; You Are Too Beautiful; I Love You Back; You Look So Good; The Resurrection Of Noah; Healing Begins With The Mind; Jubilee Worldwide; Lara, Forever; Tanisha Love; Galina, All About Love; Ekaterina, Hot and Lovely; Natalia, With Love; Svetlana, Angel Of Love; I Call My Sugar, Candie*; *Love of My Life;* and *The Second Coming!*

www.ingramcontent.com/pod-product-compliance
Lightning Source LLC
Chambersburg PA
CBHW042127080426
42734CB00001B/24